Hunger Meditations for Lent

hARVEST THE WHEAT

FLAIL THE GRAIN

tHAT ALL HOUSEHOLDERS MIGHT BAKE BREAD AGAIN

Gleanings

Edited by
Ray A. Buchanan
and
James D. Righter

Introduction
Ray A. Buchanan

GLEANINGS begins with the understanding that hunger is the greatest moral issue facing today's Christian Church. Nothing has more impact on our spirituality than what we as Christians do about daily bread.

Lent is a period rich with spiritual possibilities, and provides the perfect setting to begin a serious assessment of where we are in our response to the plight of our 500 million hungry brothers and sisters. Traditionally, the 40 days of Lent have been a time of preparation, penitence and spiritual renewal. What could be more meaningful today than to identify with the ones our Lord called "the least of these," as we prepare ourselves for the glorious celebration of Easter?

GLEANINGS also begins from the assumption that the most important changes that need to take place on behalf of the hungry are internal rather than external. The first changes have to be of our hearts, our minds, and our will. Only then will there be the sustainable power to affect the other necessary changes that must be made.

Make no mistake. The external and physical changes have to take place. The hungry and oppressed will not receive justice unless these external changes occur. But the knowledge that dramatic changes must be made is certainly no guarantee that the changes will be instituted. The simple recognition of the problems facing the hungry is but one small part of seeing that justice is done.

Recognition of the inescapable relationship between our inner spirituality and outward actions is also necessary. A great deal of the lack of action on behalf of the oppressed is due to the spiritual shallowness of our age. Only when we again come to the place where we more fully appreciate the depth of God's convenantal relationship will we be convinced we are called to share ourselves with the hungry of the world.

We must come to a place where we no longer allow ourselves to be conformed to the surrounding society, but begin to be transformed by a growing sense of God's will. We have to arrive at the place where God's hunger for justice is our daily bread. We will never deal properly with world hunger until we reach that point.

A less consumptive lifestyle should be seen as an act of faithfulness. It is an expression of personal commitment to a more equitable and just distribution of the world's resources.

Two-thirds of the human family continually lives in the shadow of starvation. A more responsible and less consumptive style of living can provide a strong bond of solidarity with those of our brothers and sisters that have no choice in the matter of lifestyle.

If we choose a more responsible lifestyle it allows us to share a greater amount of what we have received with those that so desperately need it. A just distribution of the world's resources starts with us. Are we willing to use less so that others might share what is available?

The choice of a more responsible lifestyle is a personal decision. We must recognize that such a choice will not by itself end the obscenity of world hunger. But, the choice of a more just way of living is a meaningful witness of faithfulness in our age.

The First Vital Steps

GLEANINGS is designed to help us take those vital first steps that will allow us to begin to more deeply identify with hungry brothers and sisters. Only when our identification with the poor allows us to share a measure of their pain and desperation will we have the will to act and to make many external changes that need to take place.

The beginning of the solution lies in looking at our world with the same loving compassion that motivated our Lord and in allowing ourselves to be so moved that we cannot be still until the obscenity of hunger is ended. We need to let go of our cool civility in order to feel the pain, the fear, the anger, and the desperation that fills the lives of the majority of the world's family. Only then will we have the will to act.

This book will not feed the hungry nor will it make any of the manifold changes that need to be made to bring about justice. It is but a beginning. It will be meaningful for the hungry, and for us, only in as much as we are motivated to identify with, and act on behalf of our hungry brothers and sisters.

The call of the Gospel compels us to continue or efforts. As John Wesley observed, "When we act on the light that has been given to us, more light will be given."

Now if every Christian family, while in health, would thus far deny themselves, would twice a week dine on the cheapest food, . . .faithfully calculate the money saved thereby, and give it to the poor over and above their usual donations, we should then hear no complaining in our streets, but the poor would eat and be satisfied.

John Wesley

An Invitation to the Reader

Egon W.D. Gerdes

World War II had just ended. I was a teenager in Germany, just reunited with my parents. Sowing and harvesting in 1945 had been a disaster. There were less provisions then than during the whole war. People went hungry.

We sat down for an evening meal—my parents, my younger sister and I. The meal consisted of handground grits from oats which my father and sister had stolen from a field, together with homemade syrup cooked from a few sugar beets for which my father had traded some of mother's bed linen.

The portions were dealt out. I got the most, my sister a little less, my father even less. My mother took hardly anything at all.

I finished first and asked my mother whether there was more to eat. The moment I said it I regretted my insensitivity. I should have known from the size of the portions what (in tears) she then put in words: "Sorry, boy, this was the last food we had in the house."

With that she broke down, a mother hurting from not being able to give her child requested food.

Ever since, I have come to treasure, even caress, food. I have thus come to hurt, with a passion, from waste. Even now, when I eat in a restaurant and see what is served only in order to be later thrown away, I feel I am committing a sin personally. Not only because others go hungry today as I once went hungry myself. But also, because thus, so it seems to me, we violate God's creation and what of it is entrusted into our care, our stewardship.

I have no patent solution: Who has? But I do invite you to take some time out every day and let the Word of God speak to you, ponder it and meditate on it. Maybe a little solution will come to you for a little problem. And when we put little problems and little solutions together, the grace of God can yet transform them into big solutions for big problems. At the same time may God transform our hearts, without which our lives stand little chance of being transforming, either.

Using the Meditations

The 40 meditations that follow are designed to be a part of a disciplined observance of Lent. Ideally, the meditations could be used as part of a daily miss-a-meal discipline during the Lenten period. If used in this manner, time normally used for the noon meal could instead be devoted to prayer and meditation on behalf of the hungry.

The most meaningful way to use the meditations in GLEANINGS is to covenant together with other Christians to forgo the same meal each day and spend the time in prayer and meditation. While the meditations can be profitably used by individuals wishing to use the time of Lent to increase their solidarity with their hungry brothers and sisters, a much greater benefit can be gained if the book is used as the focus for a Lenten Covenant Program.

To set up a Lenten Covenant Program for a congregation or other organization, the following guidelines will prove helpful.

1. Put hunger on the agenda of the church. The pastor should preach and teach on hunger whenever the opportunity presents itself, but especially during the Lenten Covenant Program. It is important that the congregation be taught of the tremendous amount of rich biblical material that deals specifically with the responsibilities of God's people toward the poor and hungry. The theological roots of our actions on behalf of the hungry must be stressed and clearly understood. Without a proper understanding of the integral relationship between spirituality and commitment to the hungry, the miss-a-meal program will be difficult to sustain.

2. Designate a Lenten Covenant Program leader. Ideally, this person should be a volunteer, or at least, one who is enthusiastic about the program. The leader's responsibilities include keeping a list of those signed up for the miss-a-mial Lenten Covenant Program, making sure that each one receives a copy of GLEANINGS, and keeping the entire congregation informed about the programs. The leader should also work closely with the pastor to ensure the Lenten Covenant Program receives high visibility in the worship services during Lent. The program leader should also be the person who keeps track of the money raised, making sure it reaches the designated agency or agencies.

3. Begin with a Lenten Covenant Program commitment service. There should be a special service at the beginning of the Lenten Covenant Program during which those wanting to participate are asked to sign their names on cards as a sign of commitment. This could appropriately be done as a part of a regular worship service. The signed cards could be placed in the offering plates as an act of worship. It would be helpful to make a list of all those who signed cards and make that list available to all the Lenten Covenant Program participants.

4. Decide when to miss-a-meal. The ideal way for the Lenten Covenant Program to work is for all the participants to agree to forgo the same meal. There is a sense of commonality when all the participants are meditating at the same time. For some this might not be possible, but should be attempted wherever possible. Many might also like to join with others during the time of prayer and meditation. Space should be made available in the church for those desiring to come together during this time.

5. Spend the time in prayer and meditation. The Lenten Covenant Program is designed to assist us to take the time from busy schedules to pause and reflect on the plight of the hungry in our world. Unless the time saved by missing a meal is used for prayer and meditation on behalf of our weaker brothers and sisters, the power we need for further response to hunger will not be available. The time spent in prayer and meditation is the most important aspect of the entire program.

6. Set aside the money saved by missing a meal each day. During the Lenten Covenant Program the participants should be encouraged to donate the amount normally spent on the missed meals to a specific hunger relief project. It is easiest for most people just to give a set amount ($1 to $3), for each meal missed. If possible, special containers or specially printed "World Hunger/Lenten Covenant Program" envelopes should be made available to all those participating in the program.

7. Highlight the conclusion of the Lenten Covenant Program. The most meaningful way to conclude the Lenten Covenant Program is to give it special emphasis at some point during the celebration of Easter. Many congregations have Easter sunrise services and/or Easter morning breakfasts that offer unique opportunities for celebrating the conclusion of the miss-a-meal program. It is also appropriate to include the conclusion of the program in the regular Easter morning worship service. Whatever else is done, time needs to be given for a special offering and dedication of the money set aside during the program.

Gleanings

Egon W.D. Gerdes

Then one of the elders addressed me, saying, "Who are these clothed in white robes, and whence have they come?" I said to him, "Sir, you know." And he said to me, "These are they who have come out of the great tribulation; they have washed their robes and made them white in the blood of the Lamb. Therefore are they before the throne of God, and serve him day and night within his temple; and he who sits upon the throne will shelter them with his presence. They shall hunger no more, neither thirst any more; the sun shall not strike them, nor any scorching heat. For the Lamb in the midst of the throne will be their shepherd, and he will guide them to springs of living water; and God will wipe away every tear from their eyes."

(Revelation 7:13-17)

In the Book of Revelation John sees a vast throng from all conceivable backgrounds become one in worship. As the meaning of the heavenly liturgy is explained to him, he understands that the worshipers are those who have overcome; and therefore, as a promise of God, they shall hunger no more.

With these words the writer of the Revelation takes up a prophetic theme which is also present in the Second Isaiah (49:10). There, too, it is difficult to limit the recipients and the beneficiaries of the promise. Sure, those who overcome come first (at least they come first in the perspective of the writers); It does not end there. Who can really tell who belongs to God's people? Who is included? Who is excluded?

Maybe that is why elsewhere in the Scriptures we are asked not to ask the question of "deserving" poor or of religious allegiance, but just to feed people. Precisely in the feeding, not they but we show whose we are.

The promise stands, they—whoever they are, maybe even we—shall hunger no more in the age to come. That age is being foreshadowed precisely by our feeding people wherever they are, far away or embarassingly near.

God's promise makes me restless. Are you restless, too? I have a hunch that this is a godly restlessness. At least I pray for it. Do you?

Gleanings

Dancing Toward Jerusalem

Philip Amerson

2

Woe to you that are full now, for you shall hunger. Woe to you that laugh now, for you shall mourn and weep.
(Luke 6:25)

She danced. Whirling and spinning I watched her. Our eyes met, hers sparkled. She won my heart. She looked to her mom and in mid-step sang out, "Mommy, now we have food!" Walking past her, I touched her hair and exchanged a smile. I thought of all the five-year-olds who have danced in food pantries during the past year.

I thought of the embarrassed parents, whose eyes, when I saw them, didn't sparkle. They were dull with hopelessness. . . no jobs, a ridiculous, demeaning welfare system, and a nagging awareness that their children depend on food centers for daily bread. I wondered how this little one could dance. Doesn't she know of the pain? When did I last dance for joy?

Every month 600 to 1,000 hungry people come to the food pantry at our center as a place of last resort in their search for food. At the same time our city neighborhoods are filling up with Yuppies, Buppies, and Frumpies—people with more than enough money, food and luxury. Many of these wealthy ones are Christian folks. Most of them have no idea that a few blocks from where they work or live children are dancing in food pantries.

Jesus came to earth, lived and died as a poor man— one who shared, not only his food, but also a different vision for humankind. His words suggest that some go hungry because others are greedy, some don't have jobs because others make immoral and selfish decisions.

Yet we do not despair, we are not bent low with sadness. In fact we dance for joy? Why? Those who abuse power today are not the final actors . . . they cannot shut off the stories of God's order. They cannot silence the dancing of five-year-olds any more than Herod could kill the Messiah by destroying all the young male children around Bethlehem long ago.

We see the new reign in the pirouettes of a little dancing girl with sparkling eyes!

Gleanings

The Widow's Mite

Ervin Dailey

3

Even now the axe is laid to the root of the trees; every tree therefore that does not bear good fruit is cut down and thrown into the fire." And the multitudes asked him, "What then shall we do?" And he answered them, "He who has two coats, let thim share with him who has none; and he who has food, let him do likewise." (Luke 3:9-11)

Several years ago I was in Liberia in West Africa on a mission tour. Our group stopped on Tuesday afternoon for worship services at the John Newton United Methodist Church. It was a joyous service with singing, praying, witnessing and preaching.

It came time in the service to receive the offering for women's work in the church. This was the first time. Seated next to the altar I watched as people brought their offerings.

Then I saw her . . . an elderly woman who was bent from age and hard work. From the front pew she made her way toward the altar. At the first incline she stumbled. Someone took her by the arm to help guide her. She reached the altar and felt for the offering plate.

Slowly she began to untie the handkerchief. Then carefully she took the copper coin from it and placed it in the plate. I thought to myself, you have seen the widow's mite. She gave all she had in the midst of her poverty.

That incident changed my life. Here I was living in the richest nation on the face of the earth with untold resources. God had richly blessed my life. What was I giving back for all God had so freely given me?

I knew that there had to be a way. I searched and discovered that ordinary people could do something about the needs of people in this world. God could give one opportunities to share if the person was open. People could share. They could reach out and make a difference in the lives of those who hunger. They need only start with a commitment to continue.

Gleanings

Quiet, Please
Franz Schafer

4

*He will not cry or lift up his voice, or make it heard in the
street; a bruised reed he will not break, and a dimly burn-
ing wick he will not quench; he will faithfully bring forth
justice.* (Isaiah 42:2-3)

In the foreword to a volume of sermons on texts from
the Book of Isaiah, Albrecht Goes writes, "Servants do
not make noise."

But is that right? The ministry of service is such a
serious matter, a commission from God. Shouldn't we
make so much noise that this ministry finds recognition in this world where so much injustice is done and
so many people are without a comforter?

In Isaiah 42 we read of the servant who appears as
such a helper of his people that he "will not shout nor
cry out" and that he won't make any noise in the
streets. How, then, will he gain a hearing?

The ministry of service is certainly also to be a voice
for the "bruised reeds," for broken and captive people. Should we not be advocates for weakened, disturb-
ed and insignificant folk? Doesn't our age very nearly
demand that we make noise in order to wake
humankind out of its apathy and to remind it of the
army of the poor, of those marginalized persons who
must learn to live at the edges of every society?

Yet we read about the suffering servant of God in
Isaiah that he required no spectacular effects, nor did
he appeal to the triumph of the will. It is much more
the silent persistence of the suffering servant, who in-
conspicuously, obviously does his work. The servant's
work is capable of calling forth sympathy for persons.
The servant doesn't have to make noise.

Ministry of service in the name of Jesus is characterized by this silent persistence. It may be hidden now
and again by impressive programs, but faithful and true
service is characterized by this quiet faithfulness. This
stillness maintains the divine secret of love: persons are
capable of loving without noise, but not without deeds.

Gleanings

We All Have Need

5

Keary Kincannon

Is not this the fast that I choose: to loose the bonds of wickedness, to undo the thongs of the yoke, to let the oppressed go free, and to break every yoke? Is it not to share your bread with the hungry, and bring the homeless poor into your house; when you see the naked, to cover him, and not to hide yourself from your own flesh? Then shall your light break forth like the dawn, and your healing shall spring up speedily; your righteousness shall go before you, the glory of the Lord shall be your rear guard. And the Lord will guide you continually, and satisfy your desire with good things, and make your bones strong; and you shall be like a watered garden, like a spring of water, whose waters fail not. (Isaiah 58:6-8, 11)

Lord, I don't understand. I'm frightened. You seem to be asking so much more than I am able to give. Who am I to loose the bonds of wickedness and let the oppressed go free? I am just one ordinary person.

I do give to those less fortunate than myself. I make regular donations of food, money and clothing. Must I really invite the homeless into my house? You know that many of them are mentally ill or alcoholics. I'm concerned about my family. Besides I've got my own personal and family problems.

It's not that I don't care about the poor and oppressed. I support all the right causes. I've even given up my holidays to work in a soup kitchen and staff a shelter.

I carry a lot of my own pain. My life is not what I want it to be. I am in need of great healing. Surely you're not suggesting that my gloom will only rise to light as I pour myself out for the hungry and afflicted.

There is no difference that really matters between me and the homeless bag lady on the street corner or the starving child in Africa. We are all God's creatures.

Healing will come only when we recognize our own poverty. As long as we separate ourselves from others, and think we are better than they because of our job, money, education, race, or family, there will be no room for God in our heart. God does not make these distinctions between us.

25

Gleanings

Hope

Tom (Butch) East

6

But the Lord sits enthroned for ever, he has established his throne for judgment; and he judges the world with righteousness, he judges the peoples with equity. For the needy shall not always be forgotten, and the hope of the poor shall not perish for ever. (Psalm 9:7, 8, 18)

In my presence, the father of one small child stood quietly as the mother read the letter from the water department saying that it would take $175 to have their water service restored.

After finishing the letter the mother dropped it on the floor and could only manage to groan "Oh no!" because there was no job, no source of provision for food, clothes, health needs, family recreation.

Yet almost immediately my dad came forth with a number of ideas of how things could be managed . . . all based on the hope that tomorrow will be different.

As a small child I learned from my dad that "have-nots" must have hope, or they will be crushed by despair.

As Christians we do have hope! The Psalmist tells us that, "the needy shall not always be forgotten: the hope of the poor shall not perish for ever."

Our God has made us to be instruments of hope. Let us offer ourselves to God today to be sources of hope by living the prayer of St. Francis:

Lord, make me an instrument of thy peace. Where there is hatred, let me sow love; where there is injury, pardon; where there is doubt, faith; where there is despair, hope. . .

Gleanings

Jean Horne

Come, behold the works of the Lord, how he has wrought desolations in the earth. He makes wars cease to the end of the earth; he breaks the bow, and shatters the spear, he burns the chariots with fire! "Be still, and know that I am God. I am exalted among the nations, I am exalted in the earth!" The Lord of hosts is with us; the God of Jacob is our refuge. (Psalms (46:8-11)

The psalmist reminds us of the nature of God's work: "he breaks the bow and shatters the spear. . .He makes wars cease to the end of the earth." As men and women formed in the image of God, we try to follow through on his perceived will.

We, too, work to "make wars cease." But the voice of God breaks into the psalmist's description: "Be *still* and *know* that *I* am God. *I* am exalted among the nations."

It is important for all who work and struggle daily with the political and social issues of our times to heed these words of God: "Be still. . ."

We are so busy; there is so much to be done: the hungry to feed, the oppressed to free, the poor to care for, demonstrations to lead, legislation to advocate. Yet God calls us to be still, not just to cease work and rest, but to "Be still and *know*. . ."

God calls us to be still, to quiet ourselves down so that we can know again, so that we can remember deeply within ourselves, that God is God.

"Be *still* and *know* that *I* am God." God is God. It is good to take time to be still, to be silent, to let the awareness overtake us that God—all powerful, all good, all Mystery—is with us!

What joy, strength and comfort come as we remember, in the frustration of an ongoing struggle, that the "Lord of hosts is with us; the God of Jacob is our refuge."

Gleanings

True Fasting
James M. Tongue

. . . if you pour yourself out for the hungry and satisfy the desire of the afflicted, then shall your light rise in the darkness and your gloom be as the noonday.(Isaiah 58:10)

Lent recalls the 40 days Jesus spent fasting in the wilderness and resisting temptation. There Jesus overcame Satan's ploys to keep him from the way of the cross. He returned from the wilderness strengthened and ready to follow boldly God's plan for his life.

A part of his wilderness victory involved the discipline of fasting; that is, doing without food. Through fasting he brought his body and its appetites under control.

For a century and a half, Protestant Christians have not thought much about fasting. Yet many folks fast without even knowing it. For the hungry of the world, for whom death approaches quickly, fasting is not a religious exercise but a daily cross to bear.

Our Lenten fasting can take on practical as well as spiritual significance if we sacrifice dollars we would have spent on food for ourselves to feed someone else.

When Jesus summarized the Law, it seemed fairly simple. It was to love God with all your heart, soul and mind, and to love your neighbor as yourself. (Matthew 22:37-39) Jesus taught us to love God and neighbor. When Jesus spoke of the great judgment, he concluded that the standard for such love would be thus: "And the King will answer them, 'Truly I say to you, as you did it to one of the least of these my brethren, you did it to me.' " (Matthew 25:40)

Fasting to feed others can help us keep our eyes on the goal of our high calling in Christ.

Gleanings

The First Commandment

Barbara Ross

And one of the scribes came up and heard them disputing with one another, and seeing that he answered them well, asked him, "Which commandment is the first of all?" Jesus answered, "The first is, 'Hear, O Israel: The Lord our God, the Lord is one; and you shall love the Lord your God with all your heart, and with all your soul, and with all your mind, and with all your strength.' The second is this, 'You shall love your neighbor as yourself.' There is no other commandment greater than these." And the scribe said to him, "You are right, Teacher; you have truly said that he is one, and there is no other but he; and to love him with all the heart, and with all the understanding, and with all the strength, and to love one's neighbor as oneself, is much more than all whole burnt offerings and sacrifices."

(Mark 12:28-33)

Jesus marvels at the insight of the teacher of the Law who recognizes the importance of the law that we are to love our neighbor as we love ourselves.

It is not difficult to understand why Jesus thought this commandment so important. He was after all, himself, a supreme servant of others. Loving someone else as much as we do ourselves is worth considering even apart from the importance Jesus gives it.

What would our world be like if all of us loved everyone else as we love ourselves? Could it mean that we would want the same good things of life for someone else that we want for ourselves?

Jesus taught by his example. Loving someone else means wanting for them all of the things that we want for ourselves. Nothing less will do. Loving someone else requires that we offer ourselves and our means, to do all that we can to meet another's needs.

In a world where so many go hungry, loving others as we love ourselves means providing food for those who are hungry.

During Lent we are offered the ultimate gift of love as Jesus gives his life that we too might know life eternal. How can we do anything less than love our neighbor as ourselves?

Gleanings

Across the World . . . Across the Street 10
G. Jeffery Allen

Now the Passover, the feast of the Jews, was at hand. Lifting up his eyes, then, and seeing that a multitude was coming to him, Jesus said to Philip, "How are we to buy bread, so that these people may eat?" This he said to test him, for he himself knew what he would do. Philip answered him, "Two hundred denarii would not buy enough bread for each of them to get a little." One of his disciples, Andrew, Simon Peter's brother, said to him, "There is a lad here who has five barley loaves and two fish; but what are they among so many?" Jesus said, "Make the people sit down." Now there was much grass in the place so the men sat down, in number about five thousand. Jesus then took the loaves, and when he had given thanks, he distributed them to those who were seated; so also the fish, as much as they wanted. And when they had eaten their fill, he told his disciples, "Gather up the fragments left over, that nothing may be lost." So they gathered them up and filled twelve baskets with fragments from the five barley loaves, left by those who had eaten.   (John 6:4-13)

The story of the feeding of the 5,000 is one of the most famous miracles of Jesus. In a class I once attended we were looking for possible natural explanations for this miracle. One suggestion was that upon seeing a young boy willing to share his meal, others with food willingly shared with those around them.

At the time I rejected this explanation, but I no longer discard it so easily. What greater miracle could have taken place than to have people sensitized to the needs of their neighbors—sharing with those who have little or nothing?

I once served a small church attended by people who cared for one another, and who worked hard to raise money for world hunger.

One day it came to our attention that a family with a young child, who lived within a stone's throw of the church building, had eaten no food for three days.

We must be sensitive to needs across the world, but also to those that exist across the street. If Christ can open our hearts to the hungry, there is no greater miracle than that.

35

Gleanings

Stephen Strock

Come now, you who say, "Today or tomorrow we will go into such and such a town and spend a year there and trade and get gain"; whereas you do not know about tomorrow. What is your life? For you are a mist that appears for a little time and then vanishes. Instead you ought to say, "If the Lord wills, we shall live and we shall do this or that." As it is, you boast in your arrogance. All such boasting is evil. Whoever knows what is right to do and fails to do it, for it is sin. (James 4:13-17)

Watching Lucille Ball's dramatic rendering of a bag lady in the movie "Stone Pillow," I thought how we are all alike. As Lucy winds her way up and down the streets of New York City surviving on the pods of our prodigal culture, her story reminds us that we are all just one tragedy or bad business deal from the street.

But she really is different from me, you know! My friends tell me I'm different. "If you want to be successful in life you need to circulate with the type of people you'd like to become," they say. It's not to my advantage to concern myself with bag people.

The writer of James knew the human tendency to place worldliness before godliness, and our natural yearning to be self-serving in our quest for success with the folks who are like we want to be. The New Testament tradition bids us to see things differently. "Stone Pillow" leaves us with the feeling that there are people out there who want to help the homeless, the hungry, the disposessed.

Am I such a person? Am I part of a community that could care that much? Is there room in my life for all of God's community?

We're only here for a short time, and we can't even be sure about tomorrow. One thing is certain: the bag ladies are just like us, needing dignity, hope, love, food, clothing, shelter, and a gracious Lord who has created us all to care for each other, that we might glorify God. Let us do what we do, because the Lord wills it.

Gleanings

The Nail Test

12

R. Kern Eutsler

*And when they came to the place which is called The Skull,
there they crucified him and the criminals, one on the right
and one on the left. And Jesus said, "Father, forgive them;
for they know not what they do."* (Luke 23:33-34a)

A young minister friend preached a sermon during
Lent, some years ago, on "The Nails of Christ." He
described in vivid detail the agonies of the crucifixion
and especially the blinding pain as the nails were driven
through the hands and feet of our Lord.

The worshipers were each handed a card as they
entered the church, attached to which was a large
square cut nail. As the preacher described the torment
of the crucifixion he asked each worshiper to take the
nail, place it in the palm of his/her hand and press as
hard as possible.

In a very personal way each felt in that moment a
little of what it meant to experience death by crucifixion.

We talk much about the hungry of the world. We
feel compassion for them. We are even moved to give
with some generosity for their relief; but I wonder often
if we have any appreciation of what it means to die
of starvation.

Let me suggest to you then that one of the disciplines
we might well employ this Lenten season is to fast for
24 hours, to let our stomachs get completely empty,
to feel the headaches, the stomach crampings and the
weakness that afflicts those who have nothing to eat.

If we follow such a discipline perhaps we will understand in a way we never have before what it means
to die of hunger. More important, we may realize the
plight of people who live with hunger all their lives.
It could be that we will take more seriously our responsibility for the hungry of the world.

Prayer: O gracious God our Father, help us to move
beyond our great abundance to understand in a deeper
sense the pain of the hungry of the world that we may
be moved to share as you would have us share, in the
name of Christ we pray. Amen.

Gleanings

Acts of God
Edith Varner

13

And as he was setting out on his journey, a man ran up and knelt before him, and asked him, "Good Teacher, what must I do to inherit eternal life?" And Jesus said to him, "Why do you call me good? No one is good but God alone. You know the commandments: 'Do not kill, Do not commit adultery, Do not steal, Do not bear false witness, Do not defraud, Honor your father and mother.'" And he said to him, "Teacher, all these I have observed from my youth." And Jesus looking upon him loved him, and said to him, "You lack one thing; go, sell what you have, and give to the poor and you will have treasure in heaven; and come, follow me." At that saying his countenance fell, and he went away sorrowful; for he had great possessions. (Mark 10:17-22)

I live alone on a small island in the Chesapeake Bay. Recently a severe storm struck suddenly. A quick, hard decision had to be made: evacuate or remain! Some neighbors fled. I chose to remain at home.

Winds became hurricane force. The front yard was one of few places in the area above water. The dock was two feet under water. I braced myself against the gale winds and watched the powerful waves. It was an awesome sight and I felt so helpless. Some people refer to these storms as forces of nature; insurance companies call them "acts of God."

It was getting dark and I went inside the house to light candles. For the first time in my entire life I was alone in the midst of a severe flood, with strong hurricane winds, without electricity, telephone or TV or radio—and it was night!

I went to bed to keep warm. Winds were howling and rain pounded on the roof.

I remembered the story of the rich young man who came to Jesus asking: "What must I do to receive eternal life?" I asked myself: "How do *I* keep the commandments? How much money do *I* give to the poor?" Jesus said to the rich young man: "Go, sell what you have, and give to the poor, and you will have treasure in heaven; and come, follow me." (Mark 10:21)

Gleanings

Face-To-Face With Poverty
Anne Broyles

14

We want you to know, brethren, about the grace of God which has been shown in the churches of Macedonia, for in a severe test of affliction, their abundance of joy and their extreme poverty have overflowed in a wealth of liberality on their part. For they gave according to their means, as I can testify, and beyond their means, of their own free will, begging us earnestly for the favor of taking part in the relief of the saints—and this, not as we expected, but first they gave themselves to the Lord and to us by the will of God. Now as you excel in everything—in faith, in utterance, in knowledge, in all earnestness, and in your love for us—see that you excel in this gracious work also. I say this not as a command, but to prove by the earnestness of others that your love also is genuine. For you know the grace of our Lord Jesus Christ, that though he was rich, yet for your sake he became poor, so that by his poverty you might become rich.

(2 Corinthians 8:1-5, 7-9)

Laurie was a bright 20-year-old student who read the newspaper daily, informing herself about world affairs.

When her church young adult group took a weekend trip to Tijuana, Mexico, with the Los Ninos program, it was the first time Laurie had been outside of the United States. Those few miles ventured over the border transported her into another world and a different reality.

During that weekend at Los Ninos, Laurie visited the garbage dumps where hundreds of people made their homes out of corrugated tin and cardboard.

For one day, Laurie met poverty face-to-face. "And after that, I have not been the same person. Oh, I look the same. I don't live in a garbage dump. I haven't given up all luxuries; but I do eat more simply. I try to save some of my money to give to the poor. When I read the newspaper, I think of my friends who live in that sooty dump. Foreign policy, immigration from Mexico, world hunger relief. . .all of these things affect me in a new way." This young woman's Christian compassion was nurtured in her experience among the poor of Tijuana.

Gleanings

God's Feast

James C. Logan

15

He said also to the man who had invited him, "When you give a dinner or a banquet, do not invite your friends or your brothers or your kinsmen or rich neighbors, lest they also invite you in return, and you be repaid. But when you give a feast, invite the poor, the maimed, the lame, the blind, and you will be blessed, because they cannot repay you. You will be repaid at the resurrection of the just." When one of those who sat at a table with him heard this, he said to him, "Blessed is he who shall eat bread in the kingdom of God!"   *(Luke 14:12-15)*

Jesus' favorite way of talking about the new age of God's mercy and justice (which was breaking forth in his own person and life) was a meal or a feast. As Luke tells the story, Jesus poses a rather awkward situation with this particular feast.

Then one of the guests gives what on the surface seems to be a religious response: "Blessed are those who will eat in the 'sweet by-and-by.' " Jesus wouldn't let the guest off the hook with such a piously evasive response. He follows with a simple story of God's feast and our, yes our, refusals to attend.

"I have bought a field. . ." Property, possessions, things become our preoccupation in life. Goods upon goods. A higher standard of living. Just a few more goods, and the poor can have the left overs. Soon goods become god.

"I have bought five yoke of oxen. . ." Oxen are a biblical symbol for power. We become power-hungry. Sometimes it is personal power. Sometimes it is nuclear power. We think that these will defend us and save us in the end.

"I have married a wife. . ." No one would quarrel with the concern for a sound marriage and a healthy family. But we can so center in upon our most personal of relationships that they become ends in themselves and end up in self-defeat.

The word of grace is also in the parable. The servant finally says to the host (God) "and still there is room." Still there is room for you and me in the feast of God, when we abandon our excuses and place ourselves with the dispossessed of this world.

45

Gleanings

A Cheerful Giver 16
Donald E. Struchen

The point is this: he who sows sparingly will also reap sparingly, and he who sows bountifully will also reap bountifully. Each one must do as he has made up his mind, not reluctantly or under compulsion, for God loves a cheerful giver. And God is able to provide you with every blessing in abundance, so that you may always have enough of everything and may provide in abundance for ever good work. As it is written, "He scatters abroad, he gives to the poor; his righteousness endures for ever." He who supplies seed to the sower and bread for food will supply and multiply your resources and increase the harvest of your righteousness. (2 Corinthians 9:6-10)

The writer of 2 Corinthians said, "He who sows sparingly will also reap sparingly, and he who sows bountifully will also reap bountifully. Each one must do as he has made up his mind, not reluctantly or under compulsion, for God loves a cheerful giver." (2 Corinthians 9:6-7)

Today I give thanks for the farmers who have sown bountifully the potatoes, sugar beets, soy beans and other staples that give life.

I thank God for the harvest which is so abundant that even after the fields have been harvested there is an abundance of food left.

In these moments of meditation I am grateful for those who do not give reluctantly or under compulsion, but who donate cheerfully from their fields.

I am grateful for the creativity and ingenuity of those who can see fields of food and find ways to distribute it to the hungry people of the world.

Prayer: Thank you, God, for the cheerful givers who allow their hearts to be touched by the faces of hunger as shown on television and make a contribution so empty food bowls may be filled.

Thank you also, God, for those who cheerfully give even when not confronted by compelling pictures of crying children, but who give because of their love of Christ and compassion for all God's children. Amen.

Gleanings

Sharing Food

David H. Andrews

17

By this we know love, that he laid down his life for us; and we ought to lay down our lives for the brethren. But if any one has the world's goods and sees his brother in need, yet closes his heart against him, how does God's love abide in him? Little children, let us not love in word or speech but in deed and in truth.   (I John 3:16-18)

The sights and sounds of Cairo, Egypt, were deeply disturbing to me. I was not prepared for this first visit to a large Third World city. The poverty and squalor were evident on all sides. Filth intruded everywhere. The sights and sounds and smells were all strange to my senses.

My mind searched for a spot where I might fit into this scene of turmoil as I viewed the crowded streets from the sanctuary of our air-conditioned tour bus. Even so, my first night's sleep was relatively untroubled as I settled into a comfortable motel in one of the more scenic areas of the city's fringe. The next morning I chose the bounteous "American" buffet breakfast over the more modest continental meal.

After breakfast I went out for a brief stroll along the street to pass the time until our tour bus would leave for another day of guided exposure to Egypt. As I turned a corner, the scene changed abruptly.

There a row of curbside vendors ladled out small bowls of several nondescript types of food to lines of poorly-dressed people.

One young man responded in a friendly way to my curiosity. He rose from his haunches where he was about to eat from his single small bowl, went over to a small table nearby, beckoning me: "Come, and have meal with me."

Then it struck me with moving impact that this young Moslem had reached out to me more truly in the spirit of the Lord whom I confessed than any of us who had more food than we could possibly eat.

Gleanings

Faith and Works
Ben Blevins

18

What does it profit, my brethren, if a man says he has faith but has not works? Can his faith save him? If a brother or sister is ill-clad and in lack of daily food, and one of you says to them, "Go in peace, be warmed and filled" without giving them the things needed for the body, what does it profit? So faith by itself, if it has no works, is dead. But some one will say, "You have faith and I have works." Show me your faith apart from your works, and I by my works will show you my faith. (James 2:14-18)

In so much as sitting down to write a meditation on world hunger, the connection between faith and works becomes clear. We may have faith; but if anyone we could feed is still hungry, there is something lacking. This is not to say that salvation must wait until no one hungers and thirsts; but I do think that faith must bear upon world hunger or it is not faith at all but something else.

So long as brothers and sisters are ill-clad and lacking daily bread, Christian people must find it in their hearts to respond. The words of James should sear the soul of every human being.

Contemplate the welfare of our human family. Why do a few have so much and so many have so little? This should be a great weight on our shoulders, until we do something about the injustice.

First we must see the tears in the eyes of the mother who cannot feed her child. What strength, courage and faith in God it must take to sustain her from one day to the next! What can we learn from her about the reality of hunger in our world?

People need not our pity but our help, not sorrow or guilt, but deeds of loving kindness. What good is faith if it does not bear fruit for others as well as for ourselves?

So long as the poor are with us, there will be opportunity to show Jesus our love. For just as we do it to the least brother or sister, we do it to our Lord.

Gleanings

The Difference Faith Makes   19
Helmut Nausner

. . . and from Jesus Christ the faithful witness, the first-born of the dead, and the ruler of kings on earth. To him who loves us and has freed us from our sins by his blood and made us a kingdom, priests to his God and Father, to him be glory and dominion for ever and ever. Amen.

(Revelations 1:5-6)

The great change in a person's life wrought by Jesus Christ can best be described by the word *forgiveness*. John Wesley explains our verse: "He hath washed us from the guilt and power of our sins with his own blood."

Not only are our past sins forgiven, but the power of sin is broken. This can be experienced in the present. Jesus Christ doesn't only forgive. He gives a new status in life and a new task to accomplish.

With the term "king" John Wesley combines the notion of being partakers of the present age, and heirs of His eternal kingdom. With "priest" John Wesley underlines the new biblical understanding of not sacrificing animals anymore but continually offering ourselves, a holy, living sacrifice.

With "king" and "priest" our new Christian responsibilities are indicated. As priestly people we are to tell every human creature that God loves the sinner and wants our present and eternal happiness. Or as Francis Asbury put it, "To live to God and to bring others so to do." As royal persons we are to become more and more advocates for the truth.

Being "kings" in the fellowship of Christ is not a question of political power but of truth. Becoming a witness for the truth entails political consequences; and suffering might be a result of this "royal privilege."

However, a situation may turn out, we are in fellowship with Jesus, the first-born of the dead who "stands by us and gives us strength to proclaim the word fully" (2 Timothy 4:17). Let us be ready to witness and suffer with our Lord.

Gleanings

Bread for the World
Ray W. Chamberlain, Jr.

20

They said to him, "Lord, give us this bread always."
(John 6:34)

There are some striking, powerful, haunting words in the new rock n' roll record, *Sun City*. Cliff and Hale cry out, "People are dying and giving up hope."

I can understand why people give up. Human wretchedness rarely descends deeper than when one is in the desperate throes of hungering. Every thought, every moment is consumed by dreams of food and memories of past meals.

As a missionary in Africa, I looked into the faces of people starving to death. In a thousand ways they implored, "Lord, give us this bread." They deserved it by their very existence as human beings.

Colin Morris, a missionary in Zambia, stumbled over a dead man on his front porch as he rushed off to another church conference. When they opened this stranger's body to determine the cause of death, they found grass and bits of paper in his shriveled stomach. Colin Morris declared that the starved dead man at his doorstep called the bluff of the church.

At *our* doorstep there are hungry people; and their very existence calls *our* bluff. Something is tragically wrong when we spend more on dog food than upon the hungry of the world.

The cry to the Lord for bread should echo within our very souls. The Lord depends on us to feed people. There is something incredibly exhilarating for Christians who respond in Christ's name.

Mother Teresa reminds us that "We give dying people bread because they hunger and perish not just for bread but also for love. When we hand them bread, we are also giving them love."

Our sacrifice in giving is born of compassion and is fulfilled in the joy of being Christ for others. Let's help answer that prayer: "Lord, give us bread."

55

Gleanings

G. Robert Abbott

And I sought for a man among them who should build up the wall and stand in the breach before me for the land, that I should not destroy it; but I found none.
(Ezekiel 22:30)

The hunger crisis is not just a government problem or a church problem. It is not a problem just to those without food or to those who are now committed to help. World hunger is also my problem and your problem. If just one person is going to bed hungry, or so long as one child is not receiving proper food, you and I must share the shame, the pain, and the responsibility.

As Christians, our commitment to help those who are hungry is rooted in God's Word. God has asked us to take a stand—to stand in the breach—to alleviate world hunger. If we fail to get involved in solving the plight of the hungry in our own land and throughout the world, we are failing to heed God's call to act. We are disobeying Christ's great commandment to love our neighbor as we love ourselves.

The world hunger problem will begin to be resolved when each of us takes a stand, when each of us commits our personal energies to overcoming the suffering associated with hunger. Learning more about the hunger crisis, regular fasting, commitment of resources—there are many ways to get involved.

Helen Keller, a woman who knew much about pain and denial, once said, "Although the world is full of suffering, it is also full of overcoming it." God calls each of us to do our share and to stand in the breach on behalf of the world's hungry.

Gleanings

The Un-blessed
James D. Righter

*Blessed are those who hunger and thirst for righteousness,
for they shall be satisfied.* (Matthew 5:6)

I wonder at times if the Christian church across the
centuries, starting with holy Scripture itself, has not
spiritualized the faith of Jesus himself almost beyond
recognition. Nowhere is this more true than in the
beatitudes—and especially in regard to hunger and
thirst.

Suppose for the moment that Jesus actually blessed
the hungry and thirsty of the world with the promise
they shall be satisfied. If following our Lord means doing that, then Christians everywhere are straining at
gnats and swallowing camels, tithing dill and mint and
cumin, while neglecting weightier matters of the Law.

Part of our hesitation, I feel sure, in opening our ears
and eyes to the plight of the needy is that to respond
would cost us all the things that separate us from them.
No one enjoys hearing, ''Go sell what you have and
give to the poor, to come follow me.'' So we pass by
on the other side, paying as scant attention to the
Gospel as to our Lord.

If the longest journey begins with a single step, then
why not take one and then another and then another,
even if our human limits keep us from following the
Lord all the way to the logical conclusion that ''Among
you, the greatest must make himself servant of all.''

The fulcrum and lever that begin to soften and to
move the human heart are found when we realize that
Christ love may lead us to do things impossible for men
and women, but possible with God. If I do what I can,
and others what they can, surely together we can make
some difference: perhaps all the difference in the world.
Meanwhile, the poor are always with us, just as Jesus
said.

Gleanings

In the beginning was the Word, and the Word was with God, and the Word was God. He was in the beginning with God; all things were made through him, and without him was not anything made that was made. In him was life, and the life was the light of men. The light shines in the darkness, and the darkness has not overcome it.

(John 1:1-5)

Some years ago I was asked by the managing editor of a major metropolitan newspaper to write a weekly Lenten series. As my theme I selected "Words for Lent."

I've forgotten exactly which words I selected to feature. What I do remember, however, and continue to affirm is that the Word as identified in St. John 1:1 is still ours to share and at no time more meaningfully than during the Lenten season.

The Word tells us to feed the hungry and encourages us when we do so. The Word also provides the spiritual food which the hungry need equally as much as they need physical nourishment.

Lent demands sacrifice. What sacrifice can be more meaningful to both the one making the sacrifice and the one receiving the benefits of that sacrifice than the sacrifice of food or money to buy food?

Lent also involves remembrance. We must remember in whose name and under whose directive we make our sacrifices, whatever and whenever those sacrifices may be.

Lent leads toward victory, the resurrection which Christians through the centuries have celebrated by thought, word and deed.

My word for the Lenten season, then, is to call upon fellow Christians to remember the Word made flesh. Let our deeds of sacrifice be directed toward continuing to feed the hungry, no matter why they may hunger.

Gleanings

God Alone
Vilem Schneeberger

24

Father, if thou art willing, remove this cup from me; nevertheless not my will, but thine be done. *(Luke 23:42)*

The night hour on the Mount of Olives is full of secrets. One thing is clear: Jesus needed the fellowship. Therefore he goes to this place with the disciples. They were always with him, he called them to be with him, to follow him, to be his "family."

We need the fellowship one with another. To follow Jesus Christ means to join his Church, the fellowship of those who also follow him. But there are situations when we need to leave the fellowship, to "withdraw from them" and stand alone before God, in fellowship with God alone.

In decisive moments of our life this is what we have to do in order to find out what God wants us to do. The fellowship of our brothers and sisters shall help us to find this way to God, but they cannot go with us or go this way for us. So our way leads from the fellowship of the Church into the fellowship with God in order to reveal what in the world we are to do. All God's witnesses had to go this way: Abraham, Moses, the prophets, the high priest in the sanctuary.

The fellowship with men and women can be a flight from God, a hiding behind others, behind their faith. God wants to speak to us personally, to call us by name, to invite us as individuals to follow him and to do his will.

When we obey this call then everything else loses its importance and God alone becomes the goal of life. This happened when Jesus said, "Father, not my will but thine be done." This surrender to God leads us to the highest peaks of spiritual life and to the most glorious victories in real life.

Gleanings

When they had finished breakfast, Jesus said to Simon Peter, "Simon, son of John, do you love me more than these?" He said to him, "Yes, Lord; you know that I love you." He said to him, "Feed my lambs." A second time he said to him, "Simon, son of John, do you love me?" He said to him, "Yes, Lord; you know that I love you." He said to him, "Tend my sheep." He said to him the third time, "Simon, son of John, do you love me?" Peter was grieved because he said to him the third time, "Do you love me?" And he said to him, "Lord, you know everything; you know that I love you." Jesus said to him, "Feed my sheep." (John 21:15-17)

They stood together as a group. We watched them from our car; so far away, yet so close inside of us, making us ache: young and old bending, straining, picking food for others so that they themselves could survive. God, help me put a voice to my ache!

The old people tell the stories; the young listen but do not hear. The roots have died—wrenched out of their soil and left to wither. The young Indian leans against the gas pump—a glazed look on his face. No future . . .no past . . .no present. No sense of who or whose he is. I look at him with my soul, and a tear slides down my cheek—but he doesn't know or care. God, help me put feet to my tears!

She smelled of urine and sweat. Her hair was tangled and matted. Her body bent with the weight of hate and disgust from others. She was an ugly pock on the skin of humanity. No place to go. . .no one to love her. . .no one to care. Hoping only for food and a place to sleep—and mabye a touch, a smile, or a tender word. God, help me put arms around your sheep!

Only through the pure-love example of Jesus can we be change agents for God. Only in a spirit of love and understanding are we able to see that God loves the down-trodden migrant worker, the noble yet broken Native American, the lost soul of a street person.

Gleanings

When you reap your harvest in your field, and have forgotten a sheaf in the field, you shall not go back to get it; it shall be for the sojourner, the fatherless, and the widow. . . You shall remember that you were a slave in the land of Egypt; therefore I command you to do this.
(Deuteronomy 24:19a, 22)

We live in a time when people of the Earth may not live in the immediate neighborhood of fields where gleaning is possible. It is therefore a sign of God's grace when good people will glean food that would otherwise be wasted.

I've just returned from seeing people in Africa, beyond our American horizon, still captives to hunger. There is nothing growing there; hence we are all the more obligated to glean in their behalf what may be left to rot in our fields.

For the children of many Central African nations, their captivity means growing up in stark poverty. Simple food and clean water are unobtainable luxuries in their young lives.

The children of America experience a more subtle captivity disguised in the glitter and glamour of a society which consumes voraciously more than our share due us as citizens of the global village.

I point this out not to evoke guilt but compassion. Christ's love working through us is so much more powerful and redemptive than any guilt-trip we may take. We need a joyful awareness of God's love in order to share gifts of grace equally with others on the planet we already share.

When the faces of our cousins in all the countries are wrinkled in laughter instead of creased with pain, then we will begin to know the land of liberation that God has promised us all since long before the first human harvest.

Gleanings

Love Lasts
Godfrey L. Tate, Jr.

Love is patient and kind; love is not jealous or boastful; it is not arrogant or rude. Love does not insist on its own way; it is not irritable or resentful; it does not rejoice at wrong, but rejoices in the right. Love bears all things, believes all things, hopes all things, endures all things. Love never ends. . .   *(I Corinthians 13:4-8a)*

This is Paul's description of how Christian love behaves in human relationships. Of all the gifts of the Spirit, the highest and best is a love that never fails.

God's children across the face of the planet Earth cry out constantly, in human pain and need: Help! Only a lasting love can lead others to respond. We love because God first loves us in Jesus Christ; and then we are able to reach out to others in love with gifts of grace and life.

Such love is slow to lose patience and looks for a way of being constructive. It is not possessive, impressive, or overbearing. It has the good manners not to pursue selfish advantage. It does not find others unworthy or wicked, but seeks to lead others into living joyfully. Love knows no limits, no end to trust, no fading of hope. It can outlast any hardship, for it never fails.

Self-examination and confession lead to repentence in the season of Lent; nowhere is this spiritual journey more needed than when we face the world's need when surrounded by such plenty. Help feed the hungry as a new opportunity for a renewal of faith through continuing the ministry of our Lord.

The poor are always with us, as Jesus said; so we may show our love of him by reaching out to them any time we want a blessing. It is in such giving love that we discover the promise of Christ to give us new life in all its richness and wholeness. Because Christ lives in us, others may live as well. In the words of a familiar hymn, "Love so amazing, so divine, demands my life, my soul, my all."

Such love never fails. May God empower us to celebrate glorious resurrection through loving deeds toward brothers and sisters who hunger and thirst.

Gleanings

Is not this the fast that I choose: to loose the bonds of wickedness, to undo the thongs of the yoke, to let the oppressed go free, and to break every yoke? (Isaiah 58:6)

The traditional fasting of Lent reminds us of the laudable willingness of many in the American churches to give up some of the resources with which they have been blessed so that the needs of others may be met. In times of crisis American church people have often given generously, and this year is certainly no exception.

Food relief in Ethiopia, help for earthquake victims in Mexico and volcano victims in Columbia, aid for flood victims in West Virginia and hurricane victims in the Gulf states—these have all occasioned a generous outpouring of resources from the church.

The passage above reminds us that membership in the community of faith also requires something more of us. It was written at a time after the Babylonian exile when the temple and all if its ritual observances had been restored. The prophet is reminding his hearers that no matter how well they carry out the rituals of religious life it means nothing unless religious concern extends to the whole of society and the conditions under which some must live their daily lives.

Piety is not an end in itself. It is meaningful only if it motivates us to seek wholeness of life for all persons, in all times and places.

Response to human need in crisis will continue to be an important part of faithful Christian life, but it must be coupled with commitment to build a faithful and just world in which fewer people go hungry, and more people look to the next day with hope.

Those who would feed the world's hungry must address the shape of an equitable world economy, the price paid by the hungry and poor for a runaway arms race, and the hopelessness which comes from the denial of basic freedoms whether it is in Afghanistan or South Africa.

Crisis aid must be coupled with systemic work for the wholeness (shalom) God intended in creation.

Gleanings

Poverty: Is There a Solution?   **29**
Paul W. Owen

Blessed is he who considers the poor! The Lord delivers him in the day of trouble. . . .   *(Psalm 41:1)*

The vast majority of the professionals in the social welfare community today have agreed in public and private that our present welfare system cannot provide the means of escaping a life of poverty. In fact, many have concluded that the system generates the very problem it supposedly was created to cure.

The basic issue for Americans today is one of morality centering on the question of what we really think of persons. Is a person worthy enough to have a right to an adequate living simply by virtue of birth; or must that living be earned by labor and interest in a competitive economy? Do we have an obligation to share—to care—to act?

Sometimes as I think about the poor in this country and the role of the Church in current social problems, I conclude that Christians have contributed to current poverty.

I look in my Bible in vain, to try to find these words: "But first they must be deserving." What I find is the message to care for the poor, regardless.

Poverty is complex and there is no simple answer. Christians know for certain that God who created all things is still sovereign and in control—holding the world together. Such a realization can only spur us to act as good and faithful servants who are concerned and who do not lose hope. God can redeem any situation.

Gleanings

Serving God and Neighbor

Jose L. Palos

When he had washed their feet, and taken his garments, and resumed his place, he said to them, "Do you know what I have done to you? You call me Teacher and Lord; and you are right, for so I am. If I then, your Lord and Teacher have washed your feet, you also ought to wash one another's feet. For I have given you an example that you also should do as I have done to you."(John 13:12-15)

What a surprising confusion it must have caused for the disciples to have Jesus, their Master and Lord, wash their feet! Why did Jesus himself do this chore reserved for household servants? The disciples must have asked themselves this.

Washing of their feet was necessary for sanitary and religious reaons as they celebrated the Passover Meal. The disciples, however, could not answer the question, "Do you know what I have done to you?"

They knew he had washed their feet, even the feet of Peter who at first objected; but they did not understand what he was trying to teach them.

Washing their feet was a real need that his disciples had that night, and Jesus himself addressed that need. He was teaching them not merely that they must wash each other's feet, but also that they as disciples must serve the real needs of others.

We live in a world today with people who are hungry. The hungry are easily found in this country and throughout the world. As Christ's disciples, Christ has called us to serve them, to take care of their needs.

To serve the hungry involves not only sharing our food with those in need, but it also means working for justice that changes the policies and situations that cause hunger in the world. Let us study, work, and pray that we might truly serve as Christ would have us serve.

Prayer: Thank you, Lord, for reminding us through this unique story that you expect us to serve others as you yourself have done. Help us now to understand what it means to serve you and our hungry neighbor today. May we do what you would want us to do. Amen.

Gleanings

And the King will answer them, "Truly, I say to you, as you did it to one of the least of these my brethren, you did it to me."   *(Matthew 25:40)*

William Borden was a dedicated missionary who gave his life for Christ in Africa. Someone said of him, "Borden kept the faith, but he did not keep it to himself."

The person who walks with God feels most strongly the urge to share that experience with others. This sharing often comes in the form of helping to alleviate suffering, or to feed the hungry, or to liberate the oppressed.

Sharing our faith is the motive behind all Christian efforts. We are under Christian imperative to go and to help do the work of Christ. Some go in person; others go through their gifts to the needy; all of us must go in our prayers and concerns.

Mahatma Gandhi is reported to have said on one occasion, "To the millions who have to go without two meals a day the only acceptable form in which God dare appear is food." What is there to say in response to such candor? We help to feed the hungry in the name of our God who has provided so abundantly and generously for us. May the season of Lent be for each of us a time for personal sacrifice and commitment to those whose hungers are far greater than ours.

Prayer: O God, make us sensitive to the needs of all your people. Out of this sensitivity motivate us to be messengers of the Christ, in whose name we pray. Amen.

Gleanings

But be doers of the word, and not hearers only, deceiving yourselves. *(James 1:22)*

Throughout the Old and the New Testament, people of faith are instructed to take care of the "widow and fatherless,"—the needy of society.

The Church has always been a benevolent institution which has sought to aid the downtrodden and despairing people of the world. In recent history, much of the benevolent work of the churches has been relinquished to world governments. The state now does what the churches have always done: care for society's needy.

At the present time the American government has asked the churches to assume more responsibility for such benevolence since budget cuts have affected the nation's poor. While the churches cannot begin to make up the millions of dollars cut back on social programs, they can help the poor in each community.

As long as Uncle Sam gets more of your money than the Lord Jesus Christ, the government will have to assume major responsibilities for the poor. If, however, the government chooses to spend more and more on defense and less on helping those in need, what can you do as a Christian?

What can your church do to meet the needs of your community? During this Lenten season of sacrifice, examine your own checkbook and examine your church's budget. How much is spent on yourself; and how much is spent on others in need? You may agree or disagree with your government's present policies. Either way, as a Christian and as a part of the Church of Jesus Christ, we should respond to the crisis of the poor among us.

Gleanings

Tempting Bread 33
Bill Kellerman

And Jesus, full of the Holy Spirit, returned from the Jordan, and was led by the Spirit for forty days in the wilderness, tempted by the devil. And he ate nothing in those days; and when they were ended, he was hungry. The devil said to him, "If you are the Son of God, command this stone to become bread." And Jesus answered him, "It is written, 'Man shall not live by bread alone.'"
(Luke 4:1-4)

On the face of it, this is a very simple temptation: Yield to hunger, make stones to bread, and break fast. Seek first one's own appetites. Be ruled by them. Join the "enemies of the cross" whose "god is their belly," as St. Paul puts it.

The runaway enormity of this temptation is written large and with a vengeance, as consumer culture. Appetites are researched, targeted, inflated, manufactured and managed. People are held in bondage by them.

To fast or deny an appetite is not some perverse self-punishment or justification. It is a prayer of freedom that loosens the bonds and restores a right relation to the created order. Yet this is so politically loaded because it breaks with the culture precisely at its up-front method of control.

The temptation stalks him relentlessly: build a movement on bread alone. Wield it as power. Following John's account of the loaves miracle, Jesus must escape to the hills lest the people come and take him by force to make him king: a bread messiah.

Mindful again of ourselves, this temptation has its triumph in the food-as-weapon side of our foreign policy. America has nearly the same corner on bread as the OPEC nations do on oil. It appears we do and will exercise that option in concert with the other instruments of global domination, putting the international squeeze on others. We beat our plowshares into swords, targeting whole nations for slow starvation and exposing the underbelly of our own consuming greed.

Against the evil power let us fast and pray. Let our bread be justice and our lives be a true sacrament.

Gleanings

At the end of forty days they returned from spying out the land. And they came to Moses and Aaron and. . . they brought back word to them and to all the congregation, and showed them the fruit of the land. And they told him, "We came to the land to which you sent us; it flows with milk and honey, and this is its fruit. Yet the people who dwell in the land are strong, and the cities are fortified and very large. . . And there we saw the Nephilim (the sons of Anak, who come from the Nephilim); and we seemed to ourselves like grasshoppers, and so we seemed to them.
(Numbers 13:25-28a, 33)

"It's too big!" "We can't handle it." "We feel powerless and so we are!" Sound familiar? Ever feel that way when facing the tragic dimensions of hunger near to home or far away?

Moses sent a group to look over the promised land. They found everything they could have hoped for. A land flowing with milk and honey. But there were also great obstacles to be reckoned with. The land was inhabited by strangers who threatened to keep the chosen people from the promise God had made.

When Caleb reported to the waiting tribes that they were well able to take their rightful place, others objected. We saw giants who will block our way, they said. ". . . and we seemed to ourselves like grasshoppers, and so we seemed to them."

How shall we overcome greed and oppression? How can we share our resources in a world that is so hostile and seems to be organized to keep people of good will in a constant state of competition and distrust?

Our emergency food pantries may run out of food. Our offerings of money may never be enough. Our efforts in public policy advocacy may not fully succeed. God does not promise us that there will be no obstacle (or giants!) to overcome.

It seems we have a choice to make. We can be like grasshoppers, or we can be God's people.

In God we live and move and have our being. Thanks be to God. Amen.

Gleanings

What does it profit, my brethren, if a man says he has faith but has not works? Can his faith save him? If a brother or sister is ill-clad and in lack of daily food, and one of you says to them, "Go in peace, be warmed and filled," without giving them the things needed for the body, what does it profit? So faith by itself, if it has no works, is dead. But some one will say, "You have faith and I have works." Show me your faith apart from your works, and I by my works will show you my faith. (James 2:14-18)

"One little boy a long time ago had two fish. One little boy a long time ago had five loaves." These are the opening phrases of "Two Fish, Five Loaves" by contemporary writers, Richard Avery and Donald Marsh. They speak not only of a familiar story from the Gospel of John, but lead us to reflect on what we have to share.

We all enjoy hearing about the little boy who went to hear Jesus teach. A large crowd of more than 5,000 people listening to Jesus grew tired and hungry. Jesus asked his followers, "How many fish and how many loaves have you got?" "Not enough to share," they responded. Then, they turned to the crowd, "How many fish and how many loaves have you got?" "Not enough to share," they replied. One small boy said, "I have two and five!" Jesus blessed what one child had to share; and there was enough for everyone.

It was a miracle for sure, but just what happened? I'm not sure I really know what the miracle was.

Is there an even greater miracle when selfish hoarding hearts are stirred to change into generous sharing spirits? Was the miracle a transformation of selfish human hearts or the increase of physical substance?

A small choir boy stands by the altar table with a basket of loaves and a jar of juice for the celebration of Holy Communion in one hand. With the other he points at people as he sings, "How many fish and how many loaves have you got? Are you willing to share or storing up carefully against some rainy day? In Jesus' plan you get a bonanza when you give what you have away."

Gleanings

A Sign of Love

36

Ray A. Buchanan

Beloved, let us love one another; for love is of God, and he who loves is born of God and knows God. He who does not love does not know God; for God is love. In this the love of God was made manifest among us, that God sent his only Son into the world, so that we might live through him. In this is love, not that we loved God but that he loved us and sent his Son to be the expiation for our sins. Beloved, if God so loved us, we also ought to love one another. No man has ever seen God, if we love one another, God abides in us and his love is perfected in us.

(1 John 4:7-12)

I was a Marine doing missionary work on special leave when I met Sue Ono. It was 1968. Her home was a single room with a thatched straw roof. Bamboo mats only partially covered the dirt floor. The most noticeable feature was the spirit of joy that pervaded the dwelling. From the moment we stooped to enter the door, the elderly lady before us never ceased to smile.

Her toothless grin grew even larger when the translator with us told her we were American Christians. She was thrilled. During our visit she even sang several Christian hymns she had only recently learned. I wasn't the only one to wipe my eyes as we listened to the familiar tune of "The Old Rugged Cross."

But it was her parting gesture that I'll always remember. Sue Ono, a transformed woman over 80 years old, was so full of love that she couldn't allow her brothers in Christ to leave without a gift. When her words were translated for us, I quickly looked around the tiny room. I saw nothing she could give. But I was wrong. I underestimated the love in Sue Ono's heart.

We walked down the beach toward our boat carrying a small jar of pickled squid and three tangerines— half of all the food in Sue Ono's hut. Sue Ono's gift was not only the kindest act I've ever experienced; it was also the clearest demonstration of Christian love I have ever witnessed.

With her selfless gift of food, Sue Ono showed me how we as disciples should live.

Gleanings

I hate, I despise your feasts, and I take no delight in your solemn assemblies. Even though you offer me your burnt offerings and cereal offerings, I will not accept them, and the peace offerings of your fatted beasts I will not look upon. Take away from me the noise of your songs; to the melody of your harps I will not listen. But let justice roll down like waters, and righteousness like an everflowing stream. (Amos 5:21-24)

Amos is saying that hunger and poverty are not historical accidents. They are the fruits of social injustice.

The poor people in Israel were exploited at both ends of the food chain. Farmers, because of indebtedness and injustice in the court, were reduced to common day laborers. What an experience: from landowners to day laborers in one lifetime.

The rich were at the same time getting richer and richer, while the poor were reduced to a state of hungry desperation.

Today, American farmers are faced with a political and economic squeeze play. In several years of droughts and bad crops, and over-extended loans, the voice of Amos rings loud anew. "I hate, I despise your feasts, and I take no delight in your solemn assemblies."

Hunger from Old Testament times to the present is the consequence of economic structures that result in the gap between the wealth and power of the rich and the helpless condition of the poor. Once set in motion, these structures of inequality tend to be self-perpetuating.

During March of 1983, I visited several West African countries. For the first time, I saw walking skeletons; wasted hopes and dreams, because of hunger. In a short time my spirit was lifted, and I saw a ray of hope. The United Methodist Church was at work. Parched grounds were bursting forth with fruits and vegetables. Because we cared—the pumps were supplying the thirsty ground with needy water. The desert of despair was becoming an oasis of hope for God's people once again.

Justice indeed will roll down like waters, and righteousness like an everflowing stream.

Gleanings

A World Without Hunger

J. Harry Haines

Then the righteous will answer him, "Lord, when did we see thee hungry and feed thee, or thirsty and give thee drink? And when did we see a stranger and welcome thee, or naked and clothe thee? And when did we see thee sick or in prison and visit thee? And the King will answer them, "Truly, I say to you, as you did it to one of the least of these my brethren, you did it to me."(Matthew 25:37-40)

During the administration of Jimmy Carter, a "Presidential Commission on World Hunger" report was released. Some 60 of America's leading economists, business, financial, political and religious leaders, joined by distinguished agronomists, carried out a worldwide survey of hunger and its root causes. Much of the analyses of why millions of people go to bed hungry every night of their lives covers familiar ground; but the conclusion of the document does propose a challenge to the United States and to the affluent West.

If these affluent nations could bring to bear on this great problem the same determination and technology that they have brought to other problems, hunger could be banished from the earth by the end of this century. There is no reason for multitudes of people to live out their lives in quiet despair with the only issue for them being one of survival.

A similar conclusion was reached some years ago at the Rome Conference on World Hunger called by the United Nations when some 120 nations gathered for two-and-a-half weeks in that city with one agenda item—to do something about world hunger. At that time the conclusions were similar except the Secretary General of the conference said: "We know how to banish hunger, and it can be done in one generation; but we do not know how to change people and systems to make it possible."

The Church of Jesus Christ has at the heart of its message that God can change people. This bold affirmation stands over against the findings of the United Nations and the Presidential Commission. The Church must be committed to be part of God's answer.

Gleanings

Take Nothing for the Journey   **39**
Rueben P. Job

And he called the twelve together and gave them power and authority over all demons and to cure diseases, and he sent them out to preach the kingdom of God and to heal. And he said to them, "Take nothing for your journey, no staff, nor bag, nor bread, nor money; and do not have two tunics. And whatever house you enter, stay there, and from there depart. And wherever they do not receive you, when you leave that town shake off the dust from your feet as a testimony against them. And they departed and went through the villages, preaching the gospel and healing everywhere.   *(Luke 9:1-6)*

I grew up in poverty. There was nothing very good or glorious about it. Poverty was a fact that influenced every day of my childhood; and certainly it is a factor in who I am today.

There was no special merit in being poor. It was a fact of life. Poverty brought few benefits then or now. If there was an advantage in being poor, it was simply this—the realization that we had nothing and in that we were creatures dependent upon the Creator. Our trust was not in things: whether our own ingenuity, wisdom, political position or wealth. Although our family was not in the church, it was clear even to us that our only hope was in God.

Luke records Jesus sending the twelve on a missionary journey. We understand fully his need to give them authority and power, as the text indicates. We are surprised at his admonition to take nothing for the journey.

Nothing for the journey? Could it be that Jesus is calling to a great reliance on community and a greater dependence upon God than we have yet realized?

If the Lenten season reminds us of anything, it surely reminds us of our dependence upon God, our interrelatedness with all humankind to repent, fast and pray. A time to take seriously the work of prayer and the inseparable bond between prayer and action.

It is also a time to let go of those idols close to our hearts that keep us from full obedience, faithful discipleship and joyful kingdom living.

Gleanings

The Spirit of the Lord God is upon me, because the Lord has anointed me to bring good tidings to the afflicted; he has sent me to bind up the brokenhearted, to proclaim liberty to the captives, and the opening of the prison to those who are bound; to proclaim the year of the Lord's favor, and the day of vengeance of our God. . . And he came to Nazareth, where he had been brought up; and he went to the synagogue, as his custom was, on the sabbath day. And he stood up to read; and there was given to him the book of the prophet Isaiah. He opened the book and found the place where it was written, "The Spirit of the Lord is upon me, because he has anointed me to preach good news to the poor. He has sent me to proclaim release to the captives and recovering of sight to the blind, to set at liberty those who are oppressed, to proclaim the acceptable year of the Lord." And he closed the book, and gave it back to the attendant, and sat down; and the eyes of all in the synagogue were fixed on him. And he began to say to them, "Today this scripture has been fulfilled in your hearing." (Isaiah 61:1-2a; Luke 4:16-21)

Jesus of Nazareth carefully and consciously chose this Scripture to announce his public ministry. He would bring the same message of hope, comfort, freedom, and covenant love of Yahweh to the enslaved Jews of his day that Isaiah brought to the Babylonian captives in his day.

Jesus therefore, in his words and work proclaimed Yahweh's freedom from all kind of slavery: freedom *from* hunger and thirst, freedom *from* anxiety over clothing and shelter, freedom *from* fear, freedom *from* loneliness, freedom *from* hate, freedom *from* oppression, and freedom *from* the prison of sin and alienation.

Why does Yahweh free slaves? So that the sons and daughters of Yahweh might be free *for* covenant love and, through their covenant love, free others.

All of us, then, who honestly bear the person of Jesus Christ, for that is the meaning of Christian, ought also to bear his message and work of freedom wherever we are and through whatever we do.

Gleanings

Beyond Prayer and Meditation

Ray A. Buchanan

Taking the time for prayer on behalf of the hungry, making the effort to meditate and listen to the mandates of the gospel on our lives is important. Yet, if we refuse to go further, we have in reality accomplished very little. As the writer of 1 John wrote, we need to love in deed and in truth, and not merely talk about it. The meditations and the lenten covenant program are but the first steps in our continuing response to the cries of the poor.

There is no simple, single magic solution to the tragedy of hunger in our world. As disciples of Christ, we are under a mandate to do all that we can to speed the day when hunger will only be a memory.

There are a number of steps that all of us need to take if we are serious about eliminating world hunger. A number of different areas need to be addressed if we hope to make a lasting impact upon the problem of the poor and of the needy.

Study

We need to commit ourselves to an intensive study of the problem of hunger. We need to explore not only hunger, but the many related issues as well. Social, political, theological, economic, scientific, and ethical questions all need to be answered if we are to deal honestly and completely with hunger.

The study in which we need to be engaged should be a part of an ongoing process of analysis, action, and reflection. We must get below the superficial "headline clipping" approach to hunger and dig deeply into the magnitude and root causes of the evil we seek to address. The true goal of our intensive study is to get us involved with more direct forms of action, allowing us to become more effective in the action we do undertake.

To be most effective, the hunger study we undertake needs to follow several different lines. Several analytical books on hunger should be read. Current newspaper and magazine articles should be read and filed for future use. It is also helpful to get on the mailing list of several public and church agencies which do hunger-related mailings.

One form of intensive study that should not be overlooked is direct observation. What is the story of hunger in our own communities? Becoming informed about the scope and nature of hunger where we live is also a necessary prelude to becoming more active in eliminating that hunger.

The formation of study and support groups on hunger is also a positive step. Often, what we cannot do alone, we can do as a group. The value of a supportive fellowship is manifold for our commitment to both study and action.

Local Hunger Involvement

Starvation is horrible. To be without food is hell. That hell is just as real when it happens in our own community as when it happens in India, Haiti, or Ethiopia. It is easy to ovelook the tragedy of hunger in our own localities. That does not mean that it doesn't exist. Most of the time it simply means we need to look a little closer.

Compared with the extent of the tragedy in Africa and other parts of the world, the problem of hunger in the United States is at first glance, almost insignificant. But, to the growing number of hungry in the United States, the hunger they experience is just as real as the hunger experienced elsewhere in the world.

Recent studies show that over 20 million citizens of the United States go hungry on a regular basis. These people are neighbors of ours. They are the elderly, living in isolation and pride, whose fixed incomes are not able to keep up with rising prices. They are the working poor, trapped by under-training and social injustice. They are the ethnic minorities, Blacks, Native Americans, Chicanos, from whose ranks come the chronically poor.

In our neighborhoods, as elsewhere in the world, the tragedy of hunger and the hell of going without food is inseparably linked to poverty. Hunger exists in the United States not because of a lack of food. It exists because of poverty.

In recent years, the growing number of hungry in our country, combined with reduced federal aid has spawned a tremendous amount of community action. This is a positive step. Almost every community now has food pantries, soup kitchens, and ecumenical service associations that have come into being to deal with the poor and hungry. All of these agencies provide numerous opportunities for us to become involved with hands-on hunger work in our own areas.

Many areas of the United States now have gleaning networks organized. Produce, normally left in the fields after harvest, is salvaged by volunteers and then distributed to the hungry. Gleaning is an excellent way to involve youth groups, civic, and service organizations in the fight against hunger.

Public Policy

There is no way for private agencies alone to fully deal with the massive tragedy of hunger and malnutrition. It is absolutely essential to the 500 million hungry of the world that Christians concerned about their plight become more involved with the food policies of the United States. The goal of a hunger-free world where no one has to go to bed hungry will never be reached until the political and economic institutions of the United States can be persuaded to make a more deliberate commitment to that goal.

The critical decisions concerning the distribution and use of the world's resources are not made in the councils of our churches. They are made in the political arena, especially at the federal level. If we are to be effective witnesses on behalf of the hungry, we must become more active in that arena. Standing together with our hungry brothers and sisters means we must become advocates on their behalf.

Active concern about the food policies of the United States is basic to our Christian faithfulness of this age. It is that simple. We must speak out for those whose voice cannot be heard. Involvement in the political arena by Christian citizens is essential in insuring that our nation's food policies are changed where necessary, and that justice is done for the hungry.

Military spending, Third World trade policies, domestic food aid, and farm policies are all areas that need critical input from informed citizens concerned with the plight of the hungry. Accurate information shared on a timely basis will impact the decisions made in the political arena. We can have a real influence on public policies if we will be faithful in using the gift of our citizenship.

Nothing has more impact on affecting public policy that direct contact with our elected representatives. When done intelligently and persistently, such contact is the basis for developing relationships that can have tremendous benefits for the hungry of our world.

Financial Support

Never before has there been such a constant flow of requests for us to help financially support the work of alleviating the ongoing tragedy of hunger. The reason for this is obvious. As the number of hungry continues to grow, the programs attempting to minister to them also grow. And the end is not in sight.

Yet, the sharing of our financial resources is one of the most tangible and obvious ways for us to help the hungry. This kind of giving is essential to the relief of immediate hunger needs.

The question that has to be raised, however, is to which requests do we respond. Where do we send our checks? What organizations will most effectively use our gifts?

Our gifts are much more effective when put into already existing church channels. The United Methodist Church and most other denominations provide many avenues for financially supporting the fight against hunger.

In the United Methodist Church there are a number of channels for hunger gifts. World Service is the basic benevolence fund. Many programs and projects funded through World Service funds strike at the basic causes of hunger. Agricultural missionaries, demonstration farms, and livestock improvement programs are a few examples of how World Service funds deal with hunger.

Advance Special giving is another excellent United Methodist channel for giving to fight hunger. Each of the three divisions of the Advance have hundreds of hunger-related programs that are supported through Advance Special funding.

An important feature of the Advance is that the total amount of each gift is received by the designated project. There is no loss due to administrative costs. This is possible because the administrative costs are already taken care of through other funds. Every cent of every dollar reaches the projects fighting hunger.

Whatever channels we use to financially support the work of eliminating hunger, good stewardship demands that we know as much as possible concerning the effectiveness of the organization seeking funds.

Lifestyle

Moving toward a more responsible lifestyle will not insure that the hungry of the world will be fed. But, the final solution to hunger is impossible as long as the citizens of the world's wealthy nations are commited to maintaining a style of life so high that is insures the majority of the world wiill remain impoverished and hungry.

As citizens of the United States we are part of a society that has demonstrated an obsession with consumption. We regularly use more economic goods than we actually need.

In the spirit of gleaning, an empty page has been provided across from each of the 40 hunger meditations for Lent. Jot there the ideas and feelings that you may experience as you study the Scripture and read what is provided as a gift to you.

Reshaping our consciousness of living in a needy world is the goal of the meditations. Our culture permits only glimpses, only fragmentary thoughts out of the corners of our minds, of what it is really like to hunger and thirst, or to live without the stuff of life. For to face human want directly is too painful, making us overwhelming conscious of all the "things" that separate haves from have-nots.

A privileged few have so much, and so many have so little. This basic injustice is not erased by all our talk about whether or not poor people are deserving, or whether or not people should help themselves. Nor does the injustice lend itself to easy solution where geopolitics keep people from addressing the common enemies of all humankind. Are we our brothers' and sisters' keepers?

The Struggle for Bread

Ray A. Buchanan

The abundant life that Jesus the Christ came to bring the world is out of the reach of the hungry. For the two-thirds of our global family held hostage to hunger there is no issue except the struggle for bread. At a minimum, one out of every eight men, women, and children on earth suffers malnutrition so severe as to shorten life, stunt physical growth, and dull mental ability.

For those who live out their entire lives in a losing struggle to find a place at the table nothing we can say will matter. As Gandhi so eloquently stated, "God himself dare not appear to a hungry man except in the form of bread." The only thing that will count is what we who are already at the table decide to do.

As followers of the one from Nazareth we have no choice except to do all in our power to see that the hungry are brought to the table. Until we are doing everything that we can to identify with and stand beside our hungry brothers and sisters, we are failing in our basic purpose of testifying to the presence of God's kingdom.

There can be no talk of evangelism without first an invitation to the table. First things must come first. If the love of God is to survive in us, the we must, as the writer of 1 John knew, begin to love in deed and truth and not just talk about it. I am convinced that we save our own souls by saving the bodies of others. We cannot continue to close our hearts to the cries of the majority of the human family. Their struggle for bread must become our struggle as well.

We must stand alongside hungry brothers and sisters to join in their struggle. Global hunger can be overcome. We just have to care enough. We also have to understand the root causes of hunger.

Root Causes of Hunger

It isn't surprising that most of us don't know the underlying causes of hunger. The enormity of 15 to 20 million of our family annually dying from hunger defies a rational approach. Instead, we have a bizaare assortment of misinformation, halftruths, and misplaced images.

The causes and roots of hunger are enormously complex, but most studies on the subject agree that there are eight major causes of global hunger. Listed very simply, and with little in the way of detailed explanation, the eight major causes are as follows:

1. **The colonial legacy:** Nations subdued other nations in order to exploit their natural resources.
2. **Business expansion:** Consumer demand in affluent nations means more exploitation of poorer (and hungry) ones by transnational corporations.
3. **Resource waste:** There is tremendous waste of food, soil, farm land, fertilizer and petroleum.
4. Agricultural errors: Wrong farming methods in the tropics and massive exportation of temperate zone technology and equipment help keep the world hungry.
5. **Rural leadership vacuum:** The colonial systems left the hungry nations with little or no real leadership as far as raising food is concerned.
6. **Urban growth:** The concentration on cities and also on industrialization in the Third World takes resources and priority away from the growth of food.
7. **Overpopulation:** There is a disparity between the population growth rate and the production of adequate food supplies. But is has been proven that insuring sufficient food for the hungry is a vital strategy for controlling the population growth.
8. **Military mania:** Preoccupation with defense spending and the arms race robs the hungry of food.

The above list represents the root causes of hunger. One or more of them will be behind all the hunger that makes the headlines or the evening news.

The Hidden Holocaust

Disasters, either natural or those caused by humans, compound the tragedy. But, the vast majority of those who die of hunger and hunger related diseases are not victims of such disasters. As tragic and newsworthy as the disasters may be, the major hunger problem of our age is not famine or starvation. Instead, it is what could be called the "hidden holocaust" of chronic malnutrition. Chronic malnutrition occurs when people consume less calories and protein than their bodies require.

Chronic malnutrition is the hidden holocaust because it works invisibly. The severe and often irreversible physical and mental damage it causes cannot immediately be observed. Shortage of calories or shortage of protein is very rarely the direct cause of death. Instead, the hidden holocaust of undernutrition kills indirectly. The victim of undernutrition becomes far more vulnerable to infectious diseases, especially those of the gastrointestinal and respiratory type. Many deaths attributed to these diseases are in reality the work of chronic malnutrition.

Poverty and the Web of Underdevelopment

The victims of undernutrition and malnutrition lack necessary food because they live in poverty. The majority of the world's hungry have neither land on which to grow their own food nor the money to buy it. The World Bank states that approximately 800 million people in the non-Socialist developing world live in such absolute poverty that they have no hope of providing themselves with even a minimally adequate diet.

It is always the poor who are hungry. Always.

Hunger is in actuality the central strand of a web of underdevelopment that includes poverty, powerlessness, low productivity, lack of education, unemployment, disease, and a high population growth rate. Hunger, as both a sympton and a source of under-development , should be the focus of our action on behalf of the poor.

Setting Our Sights

All who become involved with the hungry very quickly come to realize that there are many levels to the tragedy. None of the causes of hunger can be changed overnight. The multitude of causes are too deeply rooted in social custom and in human nature. Hunger is the largest obscenity of our age, and there is no one simple solution that will erase it.

We must just remember what our faith implies. Christ consistently identified himself with the poor and hungry. Dare we do less?

Contribution List

G. Robert Abbot, Office of the Vice President, Washington, D.C.

G. Jeffery Allen, Pastor, St. Mark's United Methodist Church, Lenexa, Kansas

Neil M. Alexander, Executive Secretary, Publishing and Interpretation, General Board of Discipleship, Nashville, Tennessee

Phil Amerson, Pastor, Broadway United Methodist Church, Indianapolis, Indiana

David H. Andrews, Council Director, Baltimore Conference, Baltimore, Maryland

C. Bruce Birch, Professor, Wesley Theological Seminary, Washington, D.C.

Robert M. Blackburn, Bishop, Richmond Area, Richmond, Virginia

Ben Blevens, High School Student, Chesterfield, Virginia

Ray Buchanan, Codirector, Society of St. Andrew, Big Island, Virginia

Anne Broyles, CoPastor, Malibu United Methodist Church, Malibu, California

Ray W. Chamberlain, Jr., Pastor, Messiah United Methodist Church, Springfield, Virginia

Ervin Daily, Field Representative, United Methodist Communications, Stone Mountain, Georgia

Tom (Butch) East, Pastor, Escatawpa United Methodist Church, Escatawpa, Mississippi

Gayla Estes, Minister, Stedman, North Carolina

R. Kern Eutsler, Bishop, Holston Area, Knoxville, Tennessee

Egon W.D. Gerdes, Pastor, Grand View United Methdist Church, Dubuque, Iowa

J. Harry Haines, Special Consultant, Church World Service, Laguna Hills, California

Jean Horne, Society of St. Andrew, Bedford, Virginia

Reuben P. Job, Bishop, Des Moines Area, Des Moines, Iowa

Bill Kellerman, Associate Pastor, Cass Community United Methodist Church, Detroit, Michigan

Keary Kincannon, Tenant Organizer, Sojourners Community, Washington, D.C.

Jan Lichenwalter, Director of Communications, Baltimore Conference, Baltimore, Maryland

James C. Logan, Professor of Theology, Wesley Theological Seminary, Washington, D.C.

John A. Lovelace, Managing Editor, *United Methodist Reporter*, Dallas, Texas

Helmut Nausner, Superintendent, Austria, Vienna, Austria

Paul W. Owen, Associate Council Director, North Alabama Conference, Birmingham, Alabama

Jose L. Palos, Council Director, Rio Grande Conference, San Antonio, Texas

James D. Righter, Associate Council Director of Communications, Virginia Conference, Richmond, Virginia

Barbara Ross, Pastor, Bolivar United Methodist Church, Bolivar, Ohio

Israel L. Rucker, Associate Council Director, Southeastern Jurisdiction, Atlanta, Georgia

Franz Schafer, Bishop, Central Conference, Zurich, Switzerland

Vilem Schneeberger, Superintendent, Czechoslovakia, Prague, Czechoslovakia

Gerald Shinn, Professor of Philosophy and Religion, University of North Carolina at Wilmington, Wilmington, North Carolina

Stephen Strock, Minister, Oxford, North Carolina

Donald E. Strutchen, Secretary of Conference Relations, Board of Global Ministries, United Methodist Church, New York, New York

Godfrey L. Tate, Jr., Director of Social and Ethnic Concerns, Virginia Conference, Richmond, Virginia

Nancy Tingle, Richmond, Virginia

James M. Tongue, Pastor, Lane Memorial United Methodist Church, Altavista, Virginia

Edith Varner, Fishing Creek, Maryland

Dorsey H. Walker, Director, Upper Sand Mountain Parish, Rainsville, Alabama

Response Blank

☐ I am interested in the ministry of the Society of St. Andrew. Please send me _____ explanatory brochures.

☐ I want to help the Society of St. Andrew fight hunger. My Lenten contribution of $_____ is enclosed.

☐ I want to support the Society of St. Andrew in an ongoing way. I pledge $_____ for 1986 which I will send in _____ installments.

☐ I want to remain informed about the ministry of the Society of St. Andrew. Please put me on your mailing list.

☐ I would like to have a representative of the Society of St. Andrew be a guest speaker.

Name_____

Address_____

City_____

State_____Zip_____

Tear out page and mail to: The Society of St. Andrew, Route 1, Box 283, Big Island, Virginia 24526.

Response Blank

☐ I am interested in the ministry of the Society of St. Andrew. Please send me _____ explanatory brochures.

☐ I want to help the Society of St. Andrew fight hunger. My Lenten contribution of $_____ is enclosed.

☐ I want to support the Society of St. Andrew in an ongoing way. I pledge $_____ for 1986 which I will send in _____ installments.

☐ I want to remain informed about the ministry of the Society of St. Andrew. Please put me on your mailing list.

☐ I would like to have a representative of the Society of St. Andrew be a guest speaker.

Name_____

Address_____

City_____

State_____Zip_____

Tear out page and mail to: The Society of St. Andrew, Route 1, Box 283, Big Island, Virginia 24526.

ACKNOWLEDGEMENTS

GLEANINGS is a community effort made possible by the cooperation and generosity of a great number of people who graciously gave of their time and talent.

The forty United Methodists who contributed meditations all took time from busy and hectic schedules. The meditations are a reflection of all our hopes for tomorrow. All the writers of the meditations deserve a special word of thanks for the unmistakable honesty of their contributions. They have shared themselves on behalf of the hungry.

The Society of St. Andrew extends its gratitude and thanks to the staff of Virginia United Methodist Communications, Inc., who helped in the publication of GLEANINGS.